HEY, GOD!
WHAT MAKES
YOU HAPPY?

ROXIE CAWOOD GIBSON

ILLUSTRATED BY

JAMES C. GIBSON

PREMIUM PRESS AMERICA
NASHVILLE, TENNESSEE

Hey, God! What Makes You Happy? by Roxie Cawood Gibson

Published by PREMIUM PRESS AMERICA

ISBN: 1-933725-78-8
ISBN 13: 978-1-933725-78-9

Library of Congress Catalog Card Number: 2006905243

PREMIUM PRESS AMERICA gift books are available at
special discounts for premiums, sales promotions, fund-
raising, or educational use. For details contact the Publisher
at P.O. Box 159015, Nashville, TN 37215, or phone toll free
(800) 891-7323 or (615)256-8484, or fax (615)256-8624.

www.premiumpressamerica.com

First Premium Press America Edition 2007
1 2 3 4 5 6 7 8 9 10

DEDICATION

This book is lovingly dedicated
to my Lord and Savior, who has
provided many "little ones" to make
me happy.

Special thanks to Paul Harvey for
his encouragement.

Roxie Gibson

God,
I've been
thinking about things
that make me happy
and that made me
wonder what makes
YOU happy.

It makes me
happy to sleep with
my teddy bear,

or play in the snow.

It makes me happy
to call my
Grandmother.

It makes
Grandmother happy
too.

It makes me happy
to swing high!

I'm happy when I
feed the piggy,

or
ride
my
bike.

It makes me happy
when I give my dog
a bone.

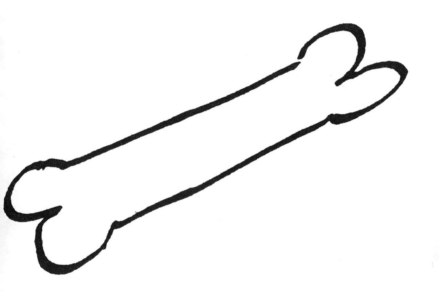

It makes me happy
to write to a friend,

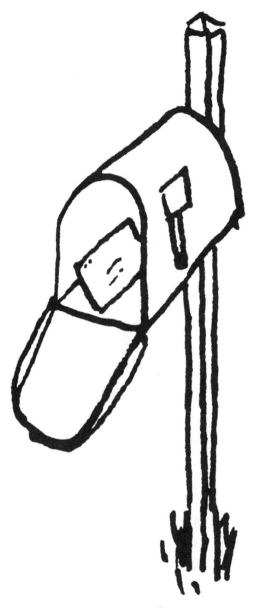

or
to
hold
hands.

It makes me happy
to learn new words.

I like to get up early,

or sleep late
sometimes.

I'm happy when
I get to go fishing,

or build
sand castles.

I'm
happy
when I laugh a lot.

It makes me happy
to find cloud
pictures,

or look for angels,

and to go bird
watching,

and hear
the birds singing.

It makes me happy
to say "the pledge,"

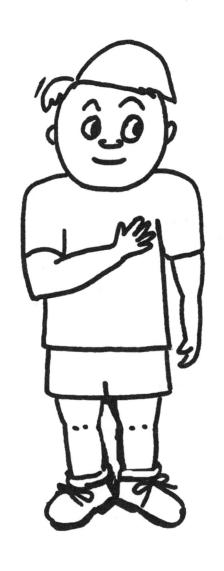

and to go to church.

But most of all, God, it makes me happy to know that God loves me just like I am!

And You know
something, God?
I believe it makes
YOU happy
when I think good
thoughts,

and when I obey
Your rules,

and honor my
Mother and Daddy,

and when I love You
and love Your other
children.

I think it makes you happy when I forgive those who are "mean" to me,

and when I correct
my mistakes,

and when I talk to
you often.

But most of all, God,
I think it makes
You happy when
I tell You I love You—
and God, I really do!